Wolfgang Amadeus

MOZART

CONCERTO

in

F MAJOR

for

PIANO

and

ORCHESTRA

KV413

MUSIC MINUS ONE

T0081725

MMO
3097

Contents

©2005 MMO Music Group, Inc. All rights reserved.
ISBN 1-59615-085-8

CONCERTO № 11
for
PIANO *and* ORCHESTRA
F major ☙ F-dur
KV413

Wolfgang Amadeus Mozart
(1756-1791)

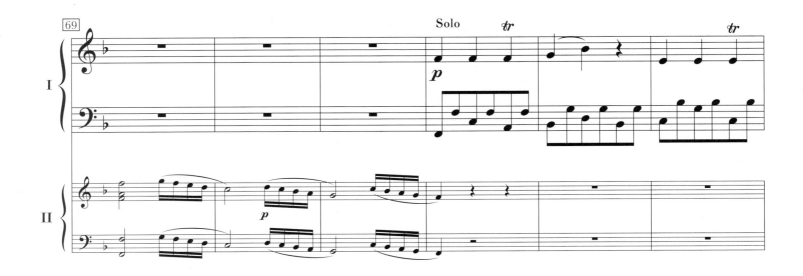

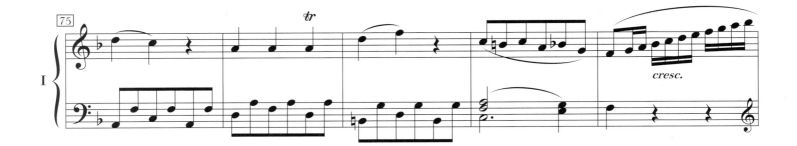

8

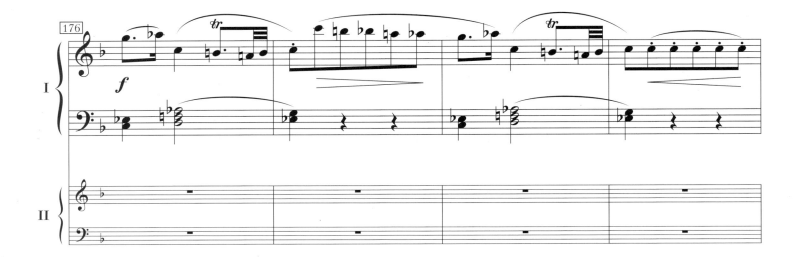

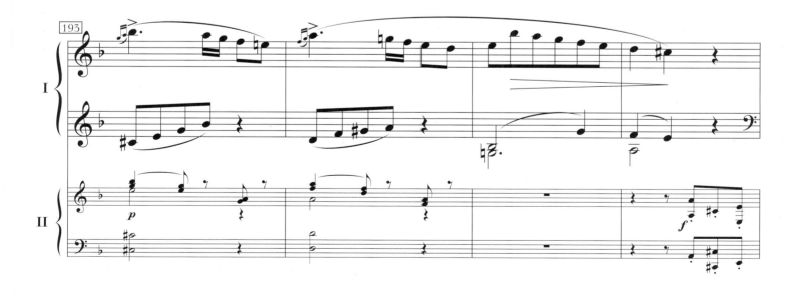

16

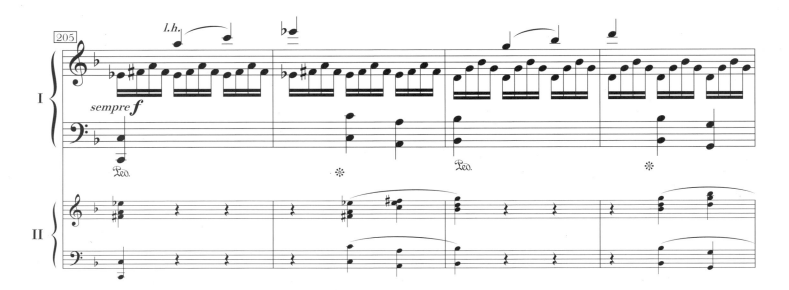

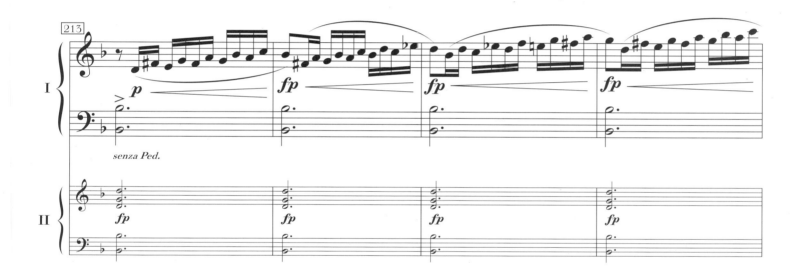

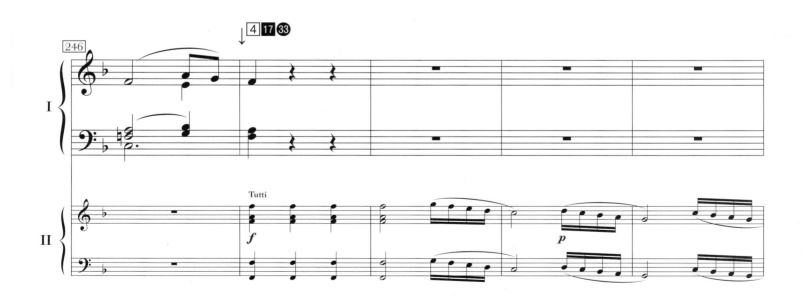

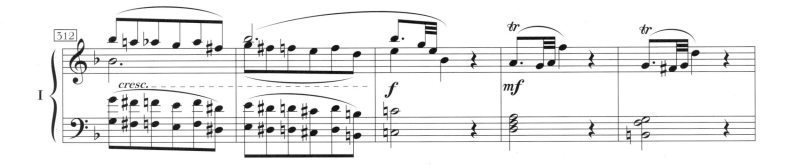

Cadenza by W.A.Mozart
non troppo allegro

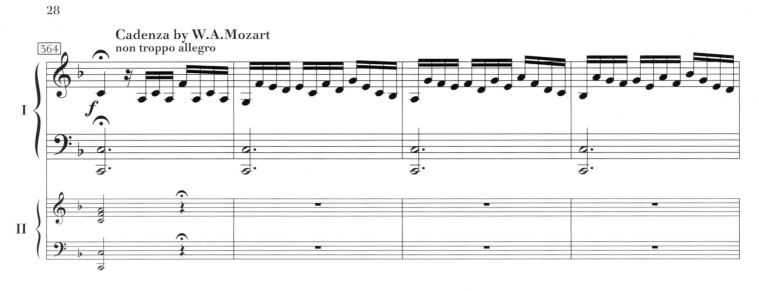

II.

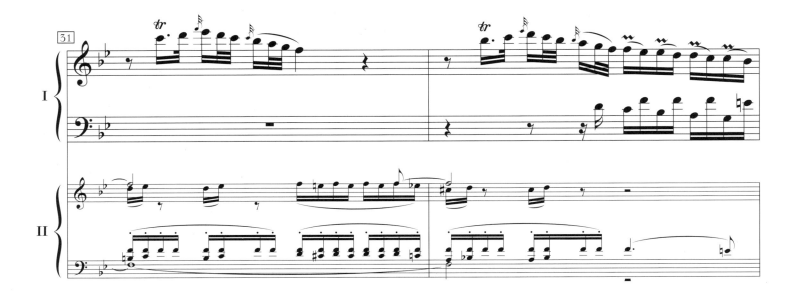

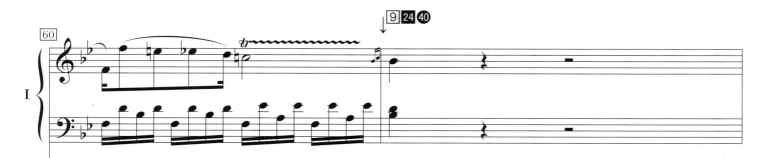

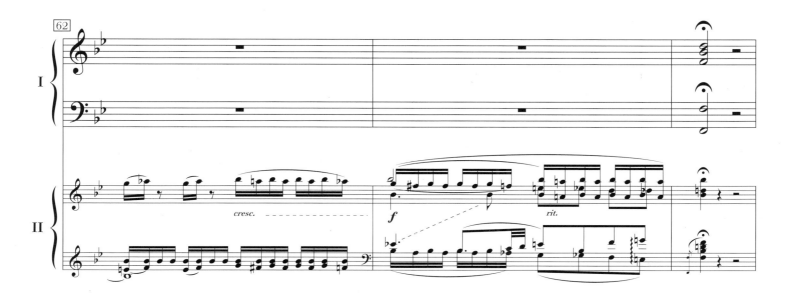

40

Cadenza by W.A.Mozart *

* The only available source is the handwriting of Leopold Mozart

MMO 3097

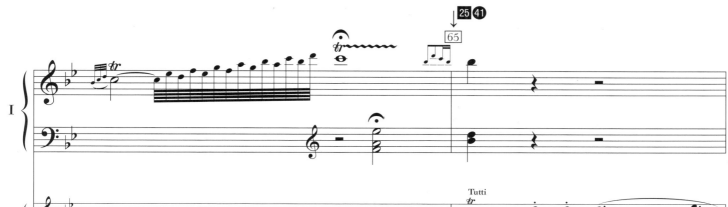

III.

44

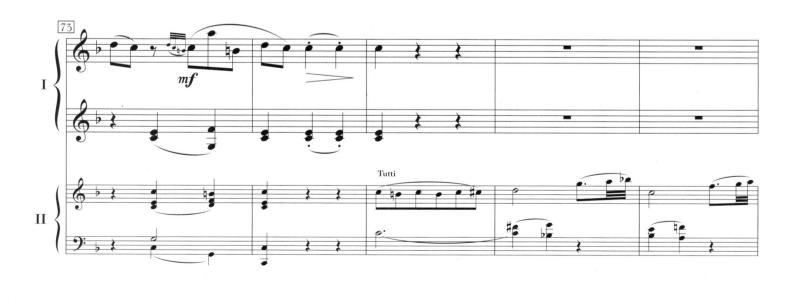

50

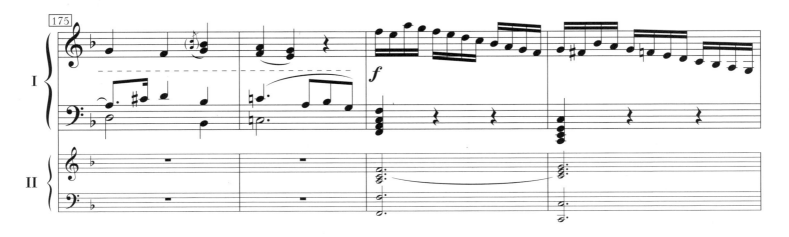

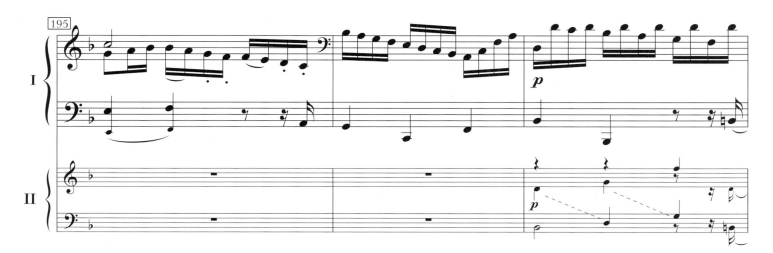

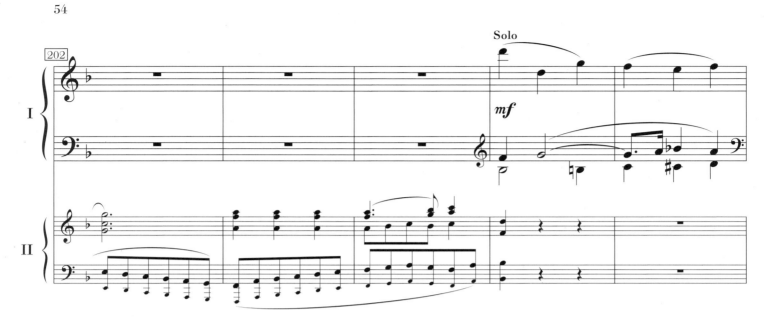

Engraving: Wieslaw Novak

SUGGESTIONS FOR USING THIS MMO EDITION

WE HAVE TRIED to create a product that will provide you an easy way to learn and perform this concerto with a full orchestra in the comfort of your own home. Because it involves a fixed orchestral performance, there is an inherent lack of flexibility in tempo and cadenza length. The following MMO features and techniques will reduce these inflexibilities and help you maximize the effectiveness of the MMO practice and performance system:

Where the soloist begins a movement *solo*, we have provided an introductory measure with subtle taps inserted at the actual tempo before the soloist's entrance.

Chapter stops on your CD are conveniently located throughout the piece at the beginnings of practice sections, and are cross-referenced in the score. This should help you quickly find a desired place in the music as you learn the piece.

Chapter stops have also been placed at orchestra entrances (e.g., after cadenzas) so that, with the help of a second person, it is possible to perform a seamless version of the concerto alongside your MMO CD accompaniment. While we have allotted what is generally considered an average amount of time for a cadenza, each performer will have a different interpretation (or in some cases substitute a different cadenza) and

observe individual tempi. Your personal rendition may preclude a perfect "fit" within the space provided. Therefore, by having a second person press the pause ❚❚ button on your CD player after the start of each cadenza, followed by the next track ▸▸❙ button, your CD will be cued to the orchestra's re-entry. When you as soloist are at the end of the cadenza or other solo passage, the second person can press the play ▸ (or pause ❚❚ button) on the CD remote to allow a synchronized orchestra re-entry.

We have observed generally accepted tempi, but some may wish to perform at a different tempo, or to slow down or speed up the accompaniment for practice purposes. In addition to the practice version included with this edition (see below), you can purchase from MMO (or from other audio and electronics dealers) specialized CD players & recorders which allow variable speed while maintaining proper pitch. This is an indispensable tool for the serious musician and you may wish to look into purchasing this useful piece of equipment for full enjoyment of all your MMO editions.

We want to provide you with the most useful practice and performance accompaniments possible. If you have any suggestions for improving the MMO system, please feel free to contact us. You can reach us by e-mail at *info@musicminusone.com*.

ABOUT THE 'PRACTICE TEMPO' VERSION

As an aid during the early stages of learning this concerto, we have created a second 'practice tempo' accompaniment recording that has been slowed by approximately 20%. This will allow you to begin at a comfortably reduced speed until fingerings and technique are more firmly in grasp, at which time the full-speed accompaniment can be substituted.

MUSIC MINUS ONE
50 Executive Boulevard
Elmsford, New York 10523-1325
1.800.669.7464 (U.S.)/914.592.1188 (International)

www.musicminusone.com
e-mail: mmogroup@musicminusone.com
